Passover Cakes
by Benny Saida

Book's desing: Ruth Rahat Studio
Photography: Philip Meteray
Illustrations: Hilla Havkin
Production & Photograph style: Bella Rodnik
Translation: Chaya Eden

Thanks for the shops: Wasershtroom - Silver Dishes,
Blue Bandana, Shigris, Tolman's

© All rights reserved by
Modan Publishing House
P.O.B. 33316, Tel-Aviv 61333
Printed in Israel, 2000

BENNY SAIDA

PASSOVER CAKES

כשר לפסח

KOSHER for PASSOVER

MODAN PUBLISHING HOUSE

contents

Almond Cake with Orange Syrup

This cake goes well with both meat and dairy menus (pareve),
and is likewise suitable for Seder night dessert.

Ingredients: Cake: ● 6 eggs, separated ● 1 cup sugar
● 9 ounces ground almonds, ● 1 tablespoon matzoh meal
Orange syrup: ● ¾ cup freshly squeezed, strained orange juice ● ½ cup sugar
● 3 tablespoons orange liqueur ● 2 cinnamon sticks
Decoration: ● sugared orange rind, sliced into thin matchsticks (optional)

10" spring-form baking pan, greased

Preparation:

1. Preheat the oven to medium heat (360 degrees F.). Whip the egg whites together with the sugar until stiff peaks form. Add the egg yolks and mix lightly. Add the almonds and the matzoh meal and mix.

2. Pour the batter into the baking pan. Bake for about 25 minutes until a toothpick inserted into the center of the cake comes out dry and clean. Let the cake cool completely.

3. Place all the syrup ingredients, including the cinnamon sticks, into a small saucepan, and bring to a boil. Cook for 3 minutes, remove the cinnamon sticks. Poke holes in the cake with a fork and pour the hot syrup over the cake. Decorate the cake with the cinnamon sticks.

4. You can also decorate the cake with slivered, sugared orange rind.
Cool the cake completely before serving.

CRUSTLESS CHEESE CAKE

Ingredients: ● 26 ounces cottage cheese, blended smooth in a blender or food processor
● 4 eggs, separated ● 3 tablespoons potato flour ● ¾ cup sugar
● 5 tablespoons instant vanilla pudding ● 1 cup sour cream
Topping: ● 1½ containers whipping cream ● 3 tablespoons sugar
● 1 pound strawberries, rinsed and drained

10" spring-form baking pan, greased

Preparation:

1. Cake preparation: Preheat the oven to medium heat (360 degrees F.). Put cheese,
egg yolks, potato flour, ½ cup sugar, pudding powder
and sour cream into a large bowl and mix well.

2. Whip the egg whites together with the remaining sugar (¼ cup) until stiff peaks form.
Fold into the cheese mixture.

3. Pour the mixture into the baking pan and bake for 1 hour until the top is golden,
or until a toothpick inserted into the center of the cake comes out dry and clean.
Slide a knife between the cake and the sides of the baking pan. Turn off the heat,
and allow the cake to cool in the oven with the door open. Cool completely.

4. Topping preparation: Whip the cream and the sugar until firm.
Spread over the cake and decorate with strawberries.

COCONUT-CHOCOLATE-RAISIN-NUT TORTE

Ingredients: ● 7 ounces butter
● 5¼ ounces semi-sweet chocolate, broken into pieces
● 3 tablespoons brandy ● 6 eggs, separated
● 1¼ cups sugar ● 5¼ ounces shredded coconut
● 3½ ounces white raisins ● 3½ ounces chopped walnuts

10″ spring-form baking pan, greased

Preparation:

1. Preheat the oven to a low heat (320 degrees F.). Place the butter and the chocolate
in a saucepan and cook over a low flame while stirring constantly until the chocolate melts.
Remove from the flame, add the brandy and egg yolks and mix well.

2. Whip the egg whites and sugar until stiff peaks form. Fold into the chocolate mixture, mixing well.
Add the remaining ingredients and mix again. Pour into the baking pan.

3. Bake for about one hour until a toothpick inserted into the
middle of the cake comes out dry and clean. Cool the cake.

BUTTERSCOTCH CAKE
WITH BRANDY SYRUP AND WHIPPED CREAM

Ingredients: Cake: ● 6 eggs, separated ● 1 cup sugar ● 4 tablespoons oil
● ½ cup matzoh cake meal ● ½ cup potato flour ● 1 tablespoon grated lemon zest
Brandy syrup: ● ½ cup sugar ● ⅓ cup water ● ¼ cup brandy
Whipped cream and decoration: ● 2 containers whipping cream ● 4 tablespoons sugar
● 7 ounces butterscotch ● toasted hazel nuts

10" spring-form baking pan, greased

Preparation:

1. Cake preparation: Preheat the oven to medium heat (360 degrees F.). Whip the egg whites with sugar until stiff peaks form. Add the egg yolks and mix lightly. Add the oil, matzoh cake meal, potato flour and lemon zest and mix well.

2. Pour the batter into the baking pan and bake for about 30 minutes. The cake is ready when a toothpick inserted into the center comes out dry and clean. Remove from oven and allow to cool while preparing the filling.

3. Syrup preparation: Put the sugar and water into a small saucepan and bring to a boil. Cook for 2 minutes and remove from the flame. Add the brandy and cool.

4. Assembling the cake: Whip the cream and sugar until firm. Remove the hoop from the spring-form baking pan. Split the cake horizontally. Place one of the halves on a serving dish and pour the syrup over it. Spread the butterscotch over the syrup and ⅓ of the whipped cream over the butterscotch.

5. Place the other half of the cake on top and spread the remaining whipped cream on the top. Decorate with the toasted hazel nuts.

Coconut Torte
WITH WHIPPED CREAM AND ALMONDS

Ingredients: ● 7 ounces softened butter ● 1 2/3 cups sugar ● 6 eggs ● 1 teaspoon grated lemon zest
● 7 ounces shredded coconut ● 1 1/2 cups matzoh cake meal
● 1/2 cup ground almonds ● 1 tablespoon baking powder
Syrup: ● 1 cup sugar ● 1/2 cup water ● 1/4 cup Amaretto liqueur (almond liqueur)
Topping: ● 2 containers whipping cream ● 4 tablespoons sugar ● 7 ounces toasted slivered almonds

10" round baking pan, greased

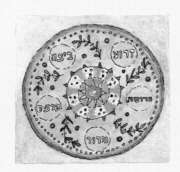

Preparation:

1. Cake preparation: Preheat the oven to medium heat (360 degrees F.). Put the butter and the
sugar in the bowl of the blender and blend for 2 minutes. Add the eggs
one by one while still blending, and blend for 3 more minutes.

2. Remove from blender to a bowl, add the lemon zest, coconut, matzoh cake meal,
almonds and baking powder and mix well by hand.

3. Pour the batter into the baking pan and bake for about 30 minutes until the top is golden and a
toothpick inserted into the center comes out dry and clean. Cool the cake completely.

4. Syrup preparation: Put the water and sugar in a small saucepan and bring to a boil.
Cook for 2 minutes and remove from the flame. Add the liqueur and mix.
Pour the hot syrup on top of the cake and cool completely.

5. Topping preparation: Whip the cream with the sugar until firm. Spread the whipped
cream over the top of the cake and decorate with toasted almond flakes.

$\mathcal{P}$ASTRY WITH COCONUT-WALNUT MERINGUE

Ingredients: Pastry: ● 6 egg yolks ● 1 cup sugar ● 1 Tablespoon brandy
● 1 tablespoon grated lemon zest ● 6 tablespoons vegetable oil
● 3 tablespoons matzoh meal ● 2 tablespoons ground almonds
● 2 tablespoons potato flour ● 1 tablespoon baking powder
Coconut merinque: ● 6 egg whites ● 1 cup sugar ● 3½ ounces grated coconut
● 3½ ounces grated semi-sweet chocolate ● 2 ounces white chocolate, grated
● ½ cup finely chopped walnuts

10″ spring-form baking pan, greased

Preparation:

1. Beat the egg yolks with sugar for about 10 minutes until light and pale yellow. Add the brandy, lemon zest and oil and mix. Heat the oven to medium heat (360 degrees F.).

2. Add the matzoh meal, ground almonds, potato flour and baking powder to the mixture and mix. Spread the dough into the baking pan.

3. Beat the egg whites and the sugar until stiff peaks form and add the remaining meringue ingredients. Spread the meringue gently on top of the dough in the baking pan.

4. Bake for about 40 minutes until the top of the meringue is golden and a toothpick inserted into the center come out clean and dry.

WALNUT-WHIPPED CREAM CAKE WITH SHAVED CHOCOLATE

Ingredients: ● 6 eggs ● 1 1/3 cups sugar ● 7 ounces ground walnuts
● 3 tablespoons matzoh meal ● 3 tablespoons brandy ● 1/4 cup freshly squeezed orange juice
Topping: ● 2 containers whipping cream ● 4 tablespoons sugar
● 3 1/2 ounces grated bitter-sweet chocolate ● 3 1/2 ounces grated white chocolate

10" spring-form baking pan, greased

Preparation:

1. Preheat the oven to medium heat (360 F.). Beat the eggs with the sugar until pale yellow and shiny. Add the walnuts, matzoh meal, brandy and orange juice and mix well.

2. Pour the batter into the baking pan and bake for about 30 minutes. Slide a knife between the cake and the sides of the baking pan and cool completely.

3. Whip the cream and the sugar until firm. Spread the whipped cream on the cake and decorate the outer rim of the cake with the white and bitter-sweet chocolate. Keep refrigerated until served.

✽ To make a layer cake: Split the cake horizontally, moisten with a little orange liqueur and spread 1/3 of the whipped cream between the cake halves.

*I*TALIAN ALMOND CAKE WITH VANILLA SAUCE

Ingredients: Cake: ● 8 egg whites ● 1¼ cups sugar ● 10½ ounces ground, blanched almonds ● 1 tablespoon grated lemon zest ● 6 tablespoons potato flour ● 2 tablespoons brandy
Vanilla sauce: ● 5 egg yolks ● ¾ cup sugar ● 2 cups milk ● 1 vanilla stick

10" spring-form baking pan, greased

Preparation:

1. Cake preparation: Preheat oven to medium heat (360 degrees F.). Whip the egg whites and the sugar until stiff peaks form. Fold in almonds gently.

2. Add lemon zest, potato flour and brandy and mix lightly.

3. Pour the mixture into the baking pan and bake for about 40 minutes.
The cake is done when a toothpick inserted into the center comes out clean and dry.
Cool and serve with the vanilla sauce on the side.

4. Vanilla sauce preparation: Beat the egg yolks and sugar until pale yellow and shiny, for about 10 minutes. Put the milk and vanilla stick in a small saucepan, bring to a boil and remove from flame. Split the vanilla stick lengthwise, and scrape the seeds into the milk.

5. Pour the milk slowly into the beaten yolks, constantly stirring. Cook over a low flame continuing to stir, until the sauce thickens (Do not allow to boil). Remove from flame.

6. Strain the sauce through a fine-meshed strainer into a bowl and stir for a minute or two. Cool, cover tightly and refrigerate until ready to serve. Serve the sauce separately with the cake.

❋ Recommendation: serve the cake accompanied by Amaretto (almond liqueur)

ALMOND CAKE WITH VANILLA SAUCE

An easy-to-prepare, unbaked almond cake enriched with whipped cream and ground walnut cookies. Serve with a cold vanilla sauce.

Ingredients: ● 2 containers whipping cream ● 2/3 cup sugar
● 5¼ ounces ground, blanched almonds
● 9 ounces walnut cookies, ground ● 4 tablespoons brandy
Decoration: ● 5¼ ounces sliced, toasted almonds
Serving: ● Vanilla sauce (see previous recipe)

8″ spring-form baking pan, greased

Preparation:

1. Whip the cream with the sugar until firm. Add the almonds, ground cookies and brandy and mix until all ingredients are combined smoothly.

2. Spread the mixture into the pan and refrigerate for at least 6 hours.

3. To serve, release the hoop from the pan and sprinkle the toasted almonds on top of the cake. Serve with vanilla sauce on the side.

Walnut Cake with Lemon Mousse Filling

Ingredients: tart: ● 14 ounces ground walnuts
● 1¼ cups sugar ● 4½ ounces melted butter
Lemon mousse: ● 5 eggs, separated ● 1 cup sugar
● ½ cup lemon juice ● 4 tablespoons frozen lemonade concentrate ● 1 tablespoon grated lemon zest
● 1 tablespoon unflavored gelatin dissolved in ⅓ cup hot water ● 2 containers whipping cream
Decoration: ● Thin strips of sugared orange and lemon peel

10″ spring-form baking pan, greased

Preparation:

1. Tart preparation: Day prior to serving: Preheat oven to medium heat (360 degrees F.)
Put all the ingredients for the tart dough into a food processor and process until the all the ingredients
are smoothly mixed and the dough is firm.

2. Spread the dough over the bottom of the baking pan with the dough, bringing it up a bit onto the
sides. Bake for about 25 minutes until the tart begins to take on a golden color.
Remove from the oven and let it cool.

3. Make the lemon mousse: Beat the egg yolks with ½ cup sugar until pale yellow and shiny. Add the
lemon juice, lemon concentrate, lemon zest and dissolved gelatin and mix.

4. In a separate bowl whip the cream until firm and fold into the beaten egg yolks.

5. In another bowl whip the egg whites with the remaining sugar (½ cup) until stiff peaks form. Fold the
whipped egg whites into the egg-lemon mixture together and mix. Spoon into the pan onto the
pre-baked tart. Refrigerate for 24 hours.

6. Decorate the top of the tart with sugared lemon and orange peel and serve.

ALMOND-WALNUT CAKE
WITH TOFFEE CREAM AND WHIPPED CREAM

Toffee cream, a mixture of caramel and whipped cream, gives this cake an especially rich flavor. Prepare the toffee cream the day before baking (two days before serving) and refrigerate for 24 hours.

Ingredients: Toffee cream: ● ½ cup sugar ● 1 container whipping cream
The cake: ● 6 eggs ● 1 cup sugar ● 7 ounces blanched, ground almonds
● 5¼ ounces ground walnuts ● 3 tablespoons vegetable oil
● 3 tablespoons brandy ● 2 tablespoons matzoh meal
Whipped cream: ● 2 containers whipping cream ● 3 tablespoons sugar
● 1 teaspoon instant coffee powder

10" spring-form baking pan, greased

Preparation:

The day before baking
1. Toffee cream: Put the sugar in a small saucepan, place over a low heat and cook, stirring constantly, until a golden caramel is obtained. Remove from the flame and slowly add the cream to the saucepan, still stirring. Return the pan to the flame, and cook until the caramel dissolves and the sauce thickens slightly. Cool and refrigerate overnight.

The day of baking
2. The cake: Preheat the oven to medium heat (360 degrees F.). Put the eggs and sugar in the bowl of the mixer and beat for 10 minutes. Add the remaining cake ingredients and mix gently.

3. Pour the batter into the baking pan and bake for about 30 minutes. The cake is ready when a toothpick inserted into the center comes out clean and dry. Cool completely.

4. Assembling the cake: Mix the toffee cream and spread over the top of the cake.

5. Whip the cream, sugar and coffee powder until firm, and spread on top of the toffee cream. Refrigerate for another 24 hours before serving.

HAZELNUT CAKE WITH HAZELNUT CREAM AND WHITE CHOCOLATE WHIPPING

Ingredients: Cake: ● 6 egg whites ● 1 cup sugar
● 4 1/2 ounces coarsely ground, toasted hazelnuts ● 3 tablespoons matzoh meal
Hazelnut cream: ● 2 containers whipping cream
● 9 ounces white chocolate, broken into small pieces
● 5 1/3 ounces coarsely ground, toasted hazelnuts
Topping: ● powdered sugar ● whole toasted hazelnuts
● a little whipped cream for decoration (optional)

9″ spring-form baking pan, greased

Preparation:

1. Cake preparation: Preheat the oven to low heat (320 degrees F.). Whip the egg whites with sugar for 5 minutes until stiff peaks form. Add the hazelnuts and the matzoh meal and mix gently.

2. Pour the mixture into the baking pan and bake for about 1 hour until the cake begins to take on a golden color. Turn off the oven. Slide a knife between the cake and the sides of the pan and return the pan to the turned-off oven for 2 hours. (It is preferable to prepare the cake the previous day and refrigerate).

3. Hazelnut cream preparation: Put the cream and chocolate in a saucepan, bring to a boil and remove from the flame. Stir until the chocolate melts. Cool and refrigerate for at least 8 hours.

4. Remove the chocolate cream from the refrigerator and whip until firm. Add the hazelnuts and mix. Spread over the cake and refrigerate.

5. Before serving sprinkle the cake with powdered sugar and decorate with whole hazelnuts. You can also decorate the cake with whipped cream rosettes.

COCONUT-LYCHEE CAKE WITH WHIPPED CREAM

Ingredients: Cake: ● 7 ounces softened butter ● 1½ cups sugar
● 8 eggs, separated ● 7 ounces shredded coconut ● ½ cup potato flour
● 1 tablespoon finely grated orange zest ● 2 tablespoons brandy
Syrup: ● ¼ cup sugar ● ½ cup water ● 4 tablespoons liqueur or brandy
Cake topping: ● 2 containers whipping cream ● 4 tablespoons sugar
● 2 cans of lychee fruit ● fresh mint leaves

10" spring-form baking pan, greased

Preparation:

1. Cake preparation: Preheat the oven to medium heat (360 degrees F.).
Put the butter and sugar into the mixer and beat for 3 minutes.
Add the egg yolks one by one while still blending, and beat for 3 more minutes.

2. Whip the egg whites to from firm peaks and fold into the yolk mixture.
Add the coconut, potato flour, orange zest and brandy and mix.

3. Pour the mixture into the baking pan and bake for about 30 minutes. The cake is done when a toothpick inserted into the center comes out dry and clean. Cool completely.

4. Syrup preparation: Put the sugar and water in a small saucepan and bring to a boil. Cook over a low flame for 5 minutes. Remove from the flame and add the liqueur or the brandy and mix.

5. Assembling the cake: Whip the cream and the sugar until firm. Drain the liquid from the lychee.

6. Split the cake horizontally and place the bottom half on a serving platter. Drip the syrup over the bottom half of the cake and spread ⅓ of the whipped cream on top. Place the upper half of the cake on top, and spread the remaining whipped cream over the surface and along the sides of the cake. Decorate with lychee fruits and mint leaves.

POPPY SEED-CHOCOLATE CAKE WITH CHERRY JAM AND WHIPPED CREAM

Ingredients: ● 3½ ounces semi-sweet chocolate, broken into pieces ● 4 ounces softened butter ● 1 cup sugar ● 6 eggs, separated ● 4½ ounces ground poppy seed ● 3 tablespoons matzoh meal
Whipped cream: ● 2 containers whipping cream ● 4 tablespoons sugar ● 3 tablespoons brandy for sprinkling ● cherry or blueberry jam
Decoration: ● Cherries, raspberries, blueberries or strawberries

9″ spring-form baking pan, greased

Preparation:

1. Preheat the oven to medium heat (360 degrees F.). Melt the chocolate in a double boiler and cool.

2. Beat the butter with ½ cup sugar until a whipped consistency is obtained. Add the egg yolks one by one while beating. Beat after each egg is added and then beat for several minutes. Add the melted chocolate and beat for 1 minute. Add the poppy seed and matzoh meal and mix by hand.

3. Whip the egg whites and remaining sugar (½ cup) to from stable peaks and fold into the chocolate mixture, mixing lightly. Pour the mixture into the baking pan and bake for about 30 minutes until a toothpick inserted into the center of the cake comes out dry and clean. Cool completely.

4. Assembling the cake: Whip the cream with 4 tablespoons of sugar until firm.
Split the cake horizontally into halves and drizzle a little brandy over the bottom half.
Spread over the cherry jam and ⅓ of the whipped cream.

5. Cover the cake with the other half and spread the remaining whipped cream on top of the cake.
Decorate with fruit.

RICH POPPY SEED CAKE
WITH WHIPPED CREAM AND WHITE CHOCOLATE

Ingredients: Cake: ● 9 ounces softened butter ● 2 cups sugar
● 10 eggs, separated ● 1 peeled apple, grated ● ¼ cup honey
● ½ cup matzoh meal ● ½ cup potato flour ● 9 ounces ground poppy seed
● 1 teaspoon baking powder ● 3½ ounces chopped walnuts
Syrup: ● ⅓ cup sugar ● ½ cup water ● ¼ orange with peel ● 1 cinnamon stick ● ¼ cup liqueur
Topping: ● 2 containers whipping cream ● 3 tablespoons sugar
● 5¼ ounces grated white chocolate

11″ spring-form baking pan, greased

Preparation:

1. Cake preparation: Preheat the oven to medium heat (360 degrees F.). Put the butter,
1 cup sugar and the egg yolks in mixing bowl and beat until shiny pale yellow.
Remove to another bowl, add the apple and the honey and mix by hand.

2. Whip the egg whites together with the remaining cup of sugar to form firm peaks.
Fold into the yolk mixture. Add the remaining cake ingredients and mix.

3. Pour the batter into the baking pan and bake for 50-60 minutes. The cake is ready when a toothpick
inserted into the center of the cake comes out dry and clean. Cool well.

4. Syrup preparation: Put all the syrup ingredients in a small saucepan except for the liqueur, and bring to
a boil. Cook for 5 minutes and strain the syrup. Add the liqueur and mix.

5. Cake assembly: Whip the cream and the sugar until stabilized. Split the cake horizontally. Place one of
the halves on a serving platter and moisten with syrup. Spread ⅓ of the whipped cream over the same
half and cover with the other cake half. Cover the top and sides of the cake with the remaining whipped
cream. Decorate with white chocolate and refrigerate until serving.

CAPPUCHINO TORTE

A coffee flavored cake, enriched with surprising flavors

Ingredients: Cake: ● 6 eggs, separated ● 2/3 cup sugar
● 7 ounces semi-sweet chocolate, broken into pieces
● 2 tablespoons brandy ● 1 heaping teaspoon Instant coffee powder
Creme filling: ● 3 1/2 ounces bitter-sweet chocolate, coarsely grated ● 2 ounces softened butter
● 2 teaspoons Instant coffee powder ● 3 eggs, separated ● 3 tablespoons sugar
Decoration: ● 2 containers whipping cream ● 1 teaspoon vanilla extract
● 1 1/2 teaspoons Instant coffee powder

9" spring-form baking pan, greased

Preparation:

1. Cake preparation: Beat the yolks and sugar until fluffy and shiny, about 8 minutes.
Melt the chocolate in the top of a double boiler and add to the yolk mixture
with brandy and coffee powder. Beat for 1 minute.

2. Preheat oven to medium heat (360 degrees F.). Whip egg whites until stiff
peaks form and fold into the chocolate mixture.

3. Pour the mixture into the baking pan and bake for about 40 minutes until a toothpick inserted into the
center comes out dry and clean. Slide a knife between the cake and the sides of the pan (after a few
minutes the cake will collapse). Cool.

4. Cream filling preparation: Melt the chocolate, butter and coffee powder in a small double boiler.
Remove from the flame, add the yolks and mix well.

5. Whip egg whites and sugar until stiff peaks form. Fold into chocolate mixture. Fill the depression in
the cake with the cream filling. Refrigerate for 6 hours.

6. Decoration: Whip the cream, vanilla and coffee powder and cover the cake with 2/3 of the whipped
cream. Fill a pastry bag with the remaining whipped cream and form rosettes on top of the cake.

CHOCOLATE-HAZELNUT-STRAWBERRY CAKE

Ingredients: Cake: ● 5 eggs, separated ● 1 cup sugar
● 8 tablespoons potato flour ● 1 teaspoon baking powder
● 4 tablespoons sweetened cocoa powder ● 2 tablespoons softened butter
Filling: ● 2 containers whipping cream ● 4 tablespoons sugar
● 3½ ounces chopped, toasted hazelnuts
Topping: ● 5¼ ounces semi-sweet chocolate, broken into pieces
● 5 eggs, separated ● 11 ounces strawberries

11" spring-form baking pan, greased

Preparation:

1. Cake preparation: Preheat oven to medium heat (360 degrees F.). Whip the egg whites and sugar until stiff peaks form. Fold the yolks gently into the whipped whites. Add the potato flour, baking powder, cocoa and butter and mix to a smooth consistency.

2. Pour the batter into the baking pan and bake for about 25 minutes until a toothpick inserted into the center of the cake comes out dry and clean. Cool well.

3. Filling preparation: Remove the hoop from the baking pan. Using a small knife, cut a large circle out of the cake, leaving a 1 inch border. Remove the upper half of the circle, and crumble into a bowl.

4. Whip the cream and the sugar until firm. Add the hazelnuts and the crumbled pieces of cake and mix well. Spoon onto the lower half of the circle and fill the empty space of the cake, pressing down well.

5. Topping preparation: Melt the chocolate in the top of a double boiler, remove from the flame, add the egg yolks and mix.

6. Whip the egg whites until stiff peaks form and fold into the chocolate mixture.

7. Place the cake on a serving platter. Spread the chocolate topping on the top and sides of the cake. Decorate with strawberries. Refrigerate for 8 hours before serving.

DELICATE CHOCOLATE CAKE

The true taste of highest quality chocolate

Ingredients: ● 7 ounces semi-sweet chocolate, broken into pieces
● ½ cup whipping cream ● 7 ounces butter
● 3 tablespoons brandy ● 6 eggs, separated ● 1 cup sugar
● 4 ounces ground walnuts ● powdered sugar for decoration.

9" spring-form baking pan, greased

Preparation:

1. Preheat the oven to medium heat (360 degrees F.). Melt the chocolate and the cream in the top of a double boiler and remove from the flame. Add butter and brandy and stir until the butter melts. Remove to a bowl and allow to cool.

2. Add the egg yolks and mix.

3. Whip the egg whites and the sugar until stiff peaks form. Fold the whites into the chocolate mixture. Add the walnuts and mix.

4. Pour the batter into the baking pan and bake for about 50 minutes until a toothpick inserted into the center comes out dry and clean. Turn off the oven, open the door of the oven and let the cake cool in the oven.

5. Decorate with the powdered sugar and serve.

CHOCOLATE EXPLOSION

A very flavorful and rich chocolate cake, without butter or whipped cream

Ingredients: ● 14 ounces semi-sweet chocolate, broken into pieces ● 1/3 cup whipping cream ● 2 tablespoons Instant coffee powder ● 4 tablespoons brandy ● 12 eggs, separated ● 1 cup sugar
Decoration: ● Bitter-sweet or white chocolate curls, or slices of kiwi

10" spring-form baking pan, greased

Preparation:

1. Put the chocolate, cream and coffee powder in the top of a double boiler and cook until the chocolate melts. Remove from the flame, add the brandy and mix.

2. Beat the egg yolks and 1/2 cup sugar until fluffy and shiny pale yellow (about 8 minutes). Add the melted chocolate mixture and beat for 1 minute. Heat the oven to medium heat (360 degrees F.).

3. Whip the egg whites and the remaining sugar (1/2 cup) until stiff peaks from. Fold the beaten whites into the chocolate/yolk mixture. Remove 1/3 of the mixture and refrigerate.

4. Pour the remaining 2/3 of the mixture into the baking pan and bake for about 30 minutes. Cool completely (when cooling, the cake will sink in the center). Spread the refrigerated 1/3 of the mixture on the cake and refrigerate for a few hours before serving. Decorate with chocolate curls or sliced kiwi.

Pavlova with Whipped Cream and Fruit

A meringue dessert filled with whipped cream and decorated with a medley of seasonal fruits.

Ingredients: Cake: ● 4 egg whites ● 1 cup sugar ● 3 tablespoons powdered sugar
● 3 tablespoons potato flour
Topping and filling: ● 2 containers of whipping cream ● 4 tablespoons sugar
● a selection of seasonal fruits (strawberries, kiwi, oranges, canned apricots)
● mint leaves for decoration

9" spring-form baking pan, greased and sprinkled with potato flour

Preparation:

1. Meringue preparation: Whip the egg whites in a mixing bowl and gradually add the sugar and the powdered sugar while beating, until stiff peaks form (about 10-15 minutes).
In the meantime heat the oven to medium-high heat (375 degrees F.).
Remove the egg whites to a bowl, add the potato flour to the whipped egg whites and mix.

2. Put the egg whites into a pastry bag with a large, star-shaped decorating tip and squeeze onto the baking pan to produce a base 1¼ inches thick. Bake for 5 minutes and lower the oven heat to 330 degrees, and bake for another 45 minutes. Turn off the oven and leave the meringue in the oven, with the oven door closed, for 4 more hours.

3. Before serving, remove the hoop from the baking pan and place the meringue on a serving platter. Whip the cream and the sugar until firm and spread the whipped cream over the meringue. Arrange the fruits on top and decorate with mint leaves. Refrigerate until ready to serve.

MERINGUE CAKE WITH WHIPPED CREAM AND STRAWBERRIES

Ingredients: ● 5 egg whites ● 1 cup sugar ● ⅓ cup powdered sugar
● 5¼ ounces ground, toasted hazelnuts
Filling: ● 3 containers of whipping cream ● 4 tablespoons sugar
● ½ teaspoon vanilla extract ● 1 pound strawberries, rinsed and dry

2 spring-form baking pans 8½" in diameter, greased, and covered with greased baking paper

Preparation:

1. Preheat the oven to medium heat (360 degrees F.). Whip the egg whites, sugar and powdered sugar to form stiff peaks. Fold the hazelnuts gently into the whipped whites. Divide into two portions.

2. Spread half of the whipped whites into each of the baking pans over the baking paper and bake each for about 40 minutes until the top of the meringue begins to take on a golden color. Cool completely.

3. Whip the cream with the sugar and the vanilla extract until firm. Clean and slice all but 12 strawberries for decoration, which remain whole, with their green leaves.

4. Carefully remove the baking paper from the bottom of the meringues. Place one meringue on a serving platter and spread on it half of the whipped cream. Arrange the sliced strawberries on the whipped cream.

5. Place the second meringue on top of the first. Spread the remaining whipped cream on top and decorate with the whole strawberries. Cool in the refrigerator for at least 5 hours before serving.

COCONUT-WALNUT MERINGUE WITH CHOCOLATE MOUSSE

Ingredients: ● 5 eggs, separated ● 1¼ cups sugar
● 7 ounces shredded coconut ● 2 ounces finely chopped walnuts
● 12¼ ounces semi-sweet chocolate, broken into pieces ● 2 containers whipping cream
● 2 tablespoons sugar ● grated zest of 1 orange
Decoration: ● grated coconut (optional)

10" spring-form baking pan, greased

Preparation:

1. The day before serving: Preheat the oven to medium heat (360 F.). Whip the egg whites and the sugar to firm peaks, add the coconut and the walnuts and mix gently.

2. Pour the mixture into the baking pan and bake for about 25 minutes until a toothpick inserted into the center of the cake comes out dry and clean. Cool well.

3. Melt the chocolate in the top of a double boiler and remove from the flame. Add the egg yolks one by one, stirring after each addition.

4. Whip the cream with 2 tablespoons sugar until firm. Add the chocolate mixture and the grated orange zest to the whipped cream. Fold gently and completely.

5. Pour the mousse onto the cake and refrigerate overnight. Decorate the cake with shredded coconut.

Hazelnut Meringue with Chocolate-Caramel Creme

Ingredients: Chocolate creme: ● 7 ounces semi-sweet chocolate, broken into pieces
● 2 containers whipping cream
Hazelnut meringue: ● 6 egg whites ● 1½ cups sugar ● 9 ounces ground, toasted hazelnuts
● 3½ ounces grated bitter-sweet chocolate ● 2 ounces grated white chocolate
Caramel: ● 1 cup sugar ● oil, for oiling

10" spring-form baking pan, greased

Preparation:

The day before baking

1. Chocolate cream preparation: Put the chocolate and the cream into a saucepan and bring to a boil while stirring until the chocolate melts. Cool and refrigerate overnight.

The day of baking

2. Meringue preparation: Preheat the oven to high heat (400 degrees F.). Whip the egg whites and the sugar together to form stiff peaks. Fold in the nuts and both chocolates, mix and spoon into the baking pan.

3. Bake for about 15 minutes until the meringue begins to take on a golden color. Slide a knife between the meringue and the sides of the pan and allow to cool.

4. Remove the cream mixture from the refrigerator, and whip until firm. Spread over the meringue.

5. Caramel preparation: Cook the sugar over medium heat until it carmelizes. Oil a work surface and pour the caramel on it. When the caramel hardens break it into small pieces with a hammer, and arrange the pieces (praline) over the top of the cake.

MERINGUE WITH HAZELNUT TRIFLE AND BRANDY MOCCA CREME

Prepare the cake the day before serving

Ingredients: Meringue: • 5 egg whites • 1 cup sugar
• 2 tablespoons sweetened cocoa powder • 3½ ounces chopped walnuts
Hazelnut trifle cream: • 14 ounces semi-sweet chocolate, broken into pieces
• 2 tablespoons chocolate liqueur • ⅓ cup whipping cream • 5 egg yolks
• 7 ounces softened butter • 3½ ounces chopped, toasted hazelnuts
Mocca-brandy creme: • 1⅔ containers of whipping cream • ¾ cup sugar
• 3 tablespoons instant coffee powder • 3 tablespoons brandy

10" baking pan, greased

Preparation:

1. Meringue preparation: The day before you plan to serve, preheat the oven to medium heat (360 degrees F.). Whip the egg whites and the sugar until stiff peaks form, about 5 minutes. Fold the walnuts and the cocoa into the whipped egg whites.

2. Pour the whipped egg whites into the baking pan and bake for 15 minutes. Lower the heat to 320 degrees F. and bake for 1 hour. Turn off the oven and slide a knife between the meringue and the sides of the pan. Return the pan to the turned-off oven for 2 hours.

3. Hazelnut trifle preparation: Put the chocolate, liqueur and cream into the top of a small double boiler and cook over boiling water until the chocolate melts. Remove from the flame, and add the egg yolks one by one, mixing constantly. Add the butter and stir. Add the hazelnuts and mix until the mousse has a uniform consistency. Place in freezer compartment of the refrigerator for 40-60 minutes, until the mousse has firmed slightly and is ready to spread.

4. Preparation of the mocca-brandy creme: Whip the cream together with the sugar until firm. Add the coffee powder and brandy and mix.

5. Assembling the cake: Spread the trifle cream over the meringue base, and the mocca cream on top of that. Refrigerate overnight.

Walnut Meringue with Chocolate Mousse and Chocolate Balls

Ingredients: Meringue: ● 5 egg whites ● 3/4 cup sugar
● 3½ ounces finely chopped walnuts ● 1 tablespoon matzoh meal
Chocolate mousse: ● ½ cup sugar ● ⅓ cup water ● 5 egg yolks
● 14 ounces semi-sweet chocolate, broken into pieces
● 4 tablespoons brandy ● 2 containers whipping cream
Decoration: ● Cocoa powder ● 12 packaged chocolate balls

10" spring-form baking pan, greased

Preparation:

1. Meringue preparation: Preheat the oven to medium heat (360 degrees F.). Whip the egg whites in a bowl and slowly add the sugar while whipping. Continue to whip until there are stiff peaks.

2. Mix the the walnuts with the matzoh meal and gently fold into the whipped eggs. Pour the mixture into the baking pan and bake for 25 minutes until the meringue begins to take on a golden color. Remove from the oven and slide a knife between the meringue and the sides of the baking pan. Let it Cool.

3. Chocolate mousse preparation: Put the sugar and water in a small saucepan and cook for about 4 minutes, until it forms a thick syrup. Remove from the flame and cool.

4. Beat the egg yolks and add the cooled sugar syrup to the beaten yolks while beating constantly. Continue to beat for about 8 minutes until the mixture is fluffy and shiny.

5. Put the chocolate and brandy in the top of a double boiler and cook until the chocolate melts, and remove from flame. Stir a bit of the melted chocolate into the yolk mixture, and then pour the yolks into the chocolate. Mix well. Allow to cool.

6. Whip the cream until firm. Slowly fold the whipped cream into the yolk-chocolate mixture, and stir well.

7. Assembling the cake: Spoon the chocolate mousse over the meringue and refrigerate until ready to serve. Before serving sprinkle the cocoa powder on the top and decorate with the chocolate balls.

PRALINE-NUT CAKE WITH CHOCOLATE MOUSSE

Ingredients: Cake: ● 3 tablespoons matzoh meal ● 3 tablespoons ground walnuts
● 2 tablespoons ground almonds ● 3 ounces grated white chocolate ● 2 tablespoons vegetable oil
● 1 teaspoon instant coffee powder
● 6 eggs, separated ● 8 tablespoons sugar
Chocolate mousse: ● 3 containers whipping cream ● 2 tablespoons sugar
● 7 ounces bitter-sweet chocolate, melted
Praline: ● oil for oiling work surface ● 1½ cups sugar
● 10½ ounces toasted hazelnuts

● ¼ cup brandy

9" spring-form baking pan, greased and lined with greased baking paper

Preparation:

1. Cake preparation: Preheat the oven to medium heat (360 degrees F.). Mix the matzoh meal, walnuts, almonds, chocolate, oil and coffee powder in a bowl.

2. In a separate bowl, whip the egg whites with the sugar until stiff peaks form.
Add the egg yolks and mix lightly to achieve a uniform consistency.
Add the mixture of matzoh meal and nuts to the egg mixture and mix.

3. Pour into the baking pan and bake for about 25 minutes. Cool well.

4. Chocolate mousse preparation: Whip the cream with the sugar until firm. Fold the melted chocolate into the whipped cream. Refrigerate.

5. Praline preparation: Oil a marble or wooden work surface. Put the sugar in a teflon-coated pan and cook over a medium heat, stirring constantly, until the sugar caramelizes.
Add the hazelnuts and mix together. Remove from the fire and pour onto the oiled surface.
Spread the mixture and let cool. Break with a hammer into small chunks.

6. Assembling the cake: Split the cake in two halves horizontally. Place one half on a serving dish and moisten with brandy. Spread half of the chocolate mousse over the brandy. Place the other cake half on top, and cover the top and the sides of the cake with the remaining chocolate mousse.

7. Decorate with chunks of the nut praline and refrigerate until ready to serve.

HAZELNUT CAKE WITH WHITE CHOCOLATE MOUSSE

Ingredients: Chocolate mousse: ● 2 containers whipping cream
● 9 ounces white chocolate, broken into small pieces
Cake ingredients: ● 8 eggs, separated ● 1¼ cups sugar
● ⅓ cup matzoh meal ● 9 ounces ground, toasted hazelnuts
● ⅓ cup Amaretto liqueur (almond liqueur), for moistening the cake
● chocolate sticks for decoration

9" spring-form baking pan, greased

Preparation:

The day before baking

1. Chocolate mousse preparation: Put the chocolate and the cream in a saucepan and bring to a boil. Stir until the chocolate melts. Remove from the flame, cool and refrigerate overnight.

The day of baking

2. Remove from refrigerator and beat until firm.

3. Cake preparation: Preheat the oven to medium heat (360 degrees F.). Whip the egg whites with the sugar until stiff peaks form. Add the yolks and mix well. Mix in the matzoh meal and the nuts.

4. Pour the batter into the baking pan and bake for about 30 minutes until a toothpick inserted in the center of the cake comes out dry and clean. Turn off the oven, open the oven door and let the cake cool in the oven.

5. Assembling the cake: Release the hoop from the baking pan. Split the cake into two halves horizontally, and place the bottom half on a serving platter. Sprinkle the liqueur on the cut side of the cake and spread a little chocolate mousse on top of the liqueur.

6. Place the second half on top of the first and spread the remaining chocolate mouse on the top and sides. Press the chocolate sticks along the sides of the cake. Cool well.

❈ Instead of chocolate sticks, try using strips of white chocolate alternated with strips of milk chocolate, both sliced from candy bars.

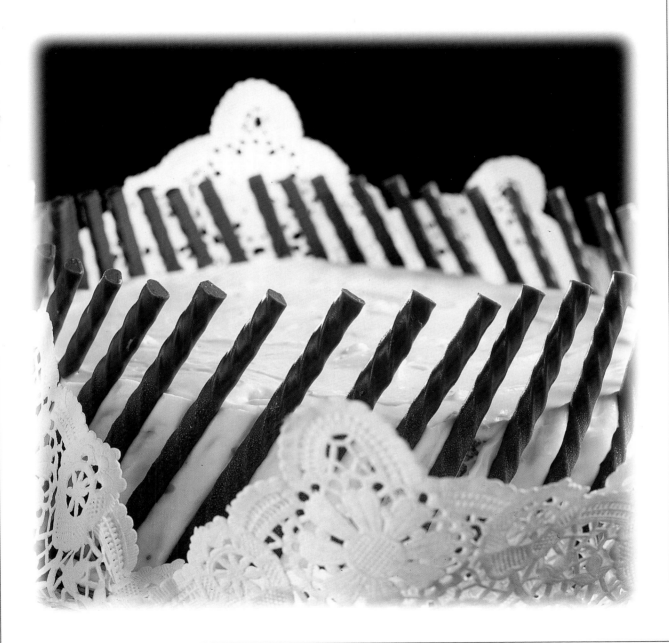

CHOCOLATE WALNUT CAKE WITH CHOCOLATE-COFFEE MOUSSE

Ingredients: Cake: ● 5¼ ounces semi-sweet chocolate, broken into pieces
● 3 tablespoons brandy ● 5 eggs, separated ● ⅔ cup sugar
● 5¼ ounces chopped walnuts ● 2 tablespoons matzoh meal
Chocolate mousse: ● 2 containers whipping cream ● 2 tablespoons powdered sugar
● 1 tablespoon instant coffee powder ● 7 ounces semi-sweet chocolate, broken into pieces, melted
Chocolate glaze: ● 3½ ounces semi-sweet chocolate chips
● 2 ounces butter ● 2 tablespoons cocoa powder
Decoration: Roasted coffee beans or chocolate coffee beans

10" spring-form baking pan, greased

Preparation:

1. Cake preparation: Preheat the oven to medium heat (360 degrees F.).
Melt the chocolate in the top of a double boiler, add the brandy and mix.

2. Whip the egg whites together with the sugar to stiff peaks, add the egg yolks and mix gently.
Add the nuts and the matzoh meal and mix. Add the chocolate/brandy mixture and mix lightly.

3. Pour into a baking pan and bake for about 35 minutes. Remove from the oven and slide a knife between the cake and the sides of the pan (the cake will have fallen a bit in the center). Cool well.

4. Chocolate mousse preparation: Whip the cream with the powdered sugar until firm.
Add the coffee powder and the melted chocolate and mix well.
Spread the mousse on the cake and refrigerate for two hours.

5. Chocolate glaze preparation: Melt the chocolate, butter and cocoa in the top of a double boiler.
Remove from heat and stir for a few minutes. Allow to cool a bit.

6. Drizzle the glaze over the cake and decorate with roasted
coffee beans or with chocolate coffee beans.

TRICOLADA CAKE

A rich cake, composed of three layers, each covered with a different chocolate.
Prepare the chocolate the day before baking (two days before serving). After preparation,
the cake is refrigerated for 24 hours before it is served.

———•·•———

Ingredients: White chocolate and halvah mousse: ● 1½ containers of whipping cream
● 2 ounces white chocolate ● 2 ounces halvah
Cake base: ● 1 tablespoon instant coffee powder ● 1 tablespoon coffee liqueur ● 3 eggs
● ⅓ cup sugar ● 2 tablespoons oil ● ½ cup matzoh cake flour
semi-sweet chocolate creme: ● ½ container whipping cream
● 7 ounces semi-sweet chocolate, broken into pieces
Milk chocolate mousse: ● 1 teaspoon unflavored gelatin ● ¼ cup boiling water
● 2 containers whipping cream ● 3 egg yolks ● ½ cup sugar ● 7 ounces milk chocolate, melted
● 1 tablespoon instant coffee powder ● 2 tablespoons brandy ● 2 egg whites

10" spring-form baking pan, oiled

Preparation:

The day before baking (two days before serving)

1. White chocolate and halvah mousse preparation: Put the cream in a saucepan
and bring to a boil over medium heat. Add the chocolate and the halvah and stir well.
Remove from flame, cool, and refrigerate for 24 hours.

The day of baking (the day before serving)

2. Cake base preparation: Preheat the oven to high heat (390 degrees F.). Dissolve the coffee
powder in the liqueur. Beat the eggs with the sugar until fluffy and shiny pale yellow.
Add the dissolved coffee, oil, matzoh meal and mix well. Pour into the baking pan and
bake for about 7 minutes. Remove from the oven and cool.

3. Chocolate cream preparation: Put the cream in a saucepan and bring to a boil. Add the chocolate and
mix until smooth. Cool, pour over the cake and refrigerate.

(cont. on page 68)

4. Milk chocolate mousse preparation: Dissolve the gelatin in the boiling water.
Whip the cream until firm.

5. In a separate bowl beat the egg yolks with ¼ cup sugar until fluffy and shiny pale yellow.
Mix in the dissolved gelatin. Add the chocolate, coffee powder and brandy and mix again.
Fold the whipped cream into the beaten egg yolks and mix lightly.

6. In another bowl, whip the egg whites with the remaining sugar (¼ cup) until stiff peaks form.
Add the whipped egg whites to the chocolate mixture and mix well.
Pour the mousse over the chocolate cream, and place in the freezer for 2 hours.

7. Beat the white chocolate and halvah mixture and spread over the milk chocolate mousse.
Refrigerate the cake for 24 hours before serving.

CHERRY CAKE
WITH THREE-FLAVORED CHOCOLATE MOUSSE

Prepare the cake and the three kinds of mousse the day before serving (see sections 1-7) and refrigerate overnight. Assemble the cake (see section 8-9) on the day of serving.

Ingredients: Cake and semi-sweet chocolate mousse: ● 3/4 cup milk
● 7 ounces semi-sweet chocolate, broken into pieces
● 7 ounces softened butter ● 3 tablespoons brandy ● 6 eggs, separated
● 1½ cups sugar ● 2 ounces chopped walnuts ● 1 peeled, grated apple
● 4 tablespoon matzoh meal ● 24 ounces pitted, canned cherries ● 4 tablespoons cherry liqueur
White chocolate mousse: ● 3½ ounces white chocolate, broken into small pieces
● 1 container whipping cream
Milk chocolate mousse: ● 1 container whipping cream
● 3½ ounces milk chocolate, broken into pieces
● 1 teaspoon Instant coffee powder
Decoration: ● 3½ ounces chopped, toasted hazelnuts

10" spring-form baking pan, greased

Preparation:

The day before serving

1. Cake preparation: Preheat the oven to low heat (300 degrees F.). Put the milk and the chocolate in a small saucepan and cook over low heat, stirring, until the chocolate melts. Remove from the flame and add the butter gradually, stirring constantly until the butter is absorbed into the chocolate. Remove to a bowl, add the brandy and the egg yolks and mix.

2. Whip the egg whites with sugar until stiff peaks form. Fold the whites into the chocolate mixture. Put 1/3 of the mixture into a glass bowl and refrigerate.

3. Add the nuts, apple and matzoh meal to the remaining chocolate mixture, mix and pour into the baking pan. Bake for about 45 minutes. Let the cake cool completely.

4. Bitter-sweet chocolate mousse preparation: Drain the cherries and mix with the mousse that has been refrigerated.

(cont. on page 70)

5. Pour the cherry liqueur over the cake. Spread the chocolate mousse/cherry mixture on top and refrigerate overnight.

6. White chocolate mousse preparation: Put the white chocolate and cream in a small saucepan and cook, stirring, until the chocolate melts. Let cool and refrigerate overnight.

7. Milk chocolate mousse preparation: Put all the mousse ingredients in a small saucepan and cook, stirring, until the chocolate melts. Let cool and refrigerate overnight.

On the day of serving

8. Remove the two mousses from the refrigerator and beat each one until stiff.

9. Assembling the cake: Spread the white chocolate mousse over the cherry-chocolate mousse that is on the cake. Refrigerate for about 3 hours until firm. Spread the milk chocolate mousse over the entire cake and sprinkle over the chopped hazelnuts. Refrigerate for 3 additional hours and serve.

Walnut Cake with Cinnamon Syrup and Crème Fraiche

Ingredients: Syrup: ● 2½ cups sugar ● 2 cups water ● 1 level teaspoon cinnamon
● juice of ½ large lemon
Cake: ● 1 cup potato flour ● 1 tablespoon baking powder
● 14 ounces ground walnuts ● 6 eggs, separated
● 1½ cups sugar ● 1 tablespoon grated lemon zest ● 1 teaspoon almond essence
Serving: 3 containers crème fraiche or rich sour cream

10″ spring-form baking pan, greased

Preparation:

1. Syrup preparation: Put the sugar, water and cinnamon in a small saucepan and bring to a boil. Add the lemon juice and cook over a low heat for 20 minutes. Cool and refrigerate.

2. Cake preparation: Mix the flour, baking powder and nuts in a bowl. Beat the yolks with 1 cup sugar until fluffy and shiny. Mix the beaten yolks into the nut mixture, add the lemon zest and almond essence and mix again.

3. Preheat the oven to medium heat (360 degrees F.). Whip the egg whites and add the remaining sugar (½ cup) gradually while beating constantly until stiff peaks form.

4. Add a few tablespoons of the whipped egg white to the yolk/nut mixture and mix. Fold in the remaining whipped egg white until uniformly mixed.

5. Pour the batter into the baking pan and bake for about 1 hour. The cake is ready when a toothpick inserted into the center comes out dry and clean.

6. Poke the cake in a few places with a fork while it is still hot. Slowly pour the cold syrup over the cake. Let the cake settle a few hours to absorb the syrup.

7. Divide the cake into portions, place a heaping tablespoon of crème fraiche next to each portion and serve.

ƒESTIVE CHOCOLATE-ORANGE CAKE

Ingredients: ● 12¼ ounces semi-sweet chocolate, broken into pieces ● 7 ounces butter
● 4 tablespoons orange liqueur ● 8 eggs, separated ● 1 cup sugar ● 1 cup orange juice
● 5¼ ounces finely ground walnuts ● 5¼ ounces finely ground hazelnuts
Topping: ● 7 ounces milk chocolate, broken into pieces ● 2 ounces butter
● 4 tablespoons whipping cream ● 2 tablespoons orange liqueur ● candied orange peel

10" spring-form baking pan, greased

Preparation:
1. Cake preparation: Preheat the oven to medium-low (340 degrees F.). Put the chocolate,
butter and liqueur in a medium saucepan and cook over a very low heat, stirring,
until the chocolate melts and the mixture is smooth. Remove from heat.

2. Beat the egg yolks, gradually adding the sugar while slowly beating. Whip for 8 more
minutes until the mixture is pale yellow and light. Add the melted chocolate to the beaten yolks,
while beating slowly. Add the orange juice slowly while continuing to beat.

3. Whip the egg whites to form stiff peaks. Add ½ of the beaten egg whites to the chocolate-yolk mixture
and mix gently. Add the remaining egg whites and the two kinds of nuts and mix well.

4. Pour the mixture into the baking pan and bake for about 1 hour until a toothpick inserted
into the center of the cake comes out dry and clean. Remove cake from the oven and cool well.
Remove the sides of the baking pan.

5. Topping preparation: Put the chocolate, butter, cream and liqueur in a small saucepan and cook over a
low heat, stirring, until the chocolate melts. Remove from fire and stir for 3 minutes.

6. Assembling the cake: To decorate the cake, place a baking rack over an empty baking pan. Put the
cake on the rack and pour the melted chocolate over the cake. Cover the top and the sides of the cake.
Refrigerate for 15 minutes.

7. Transfer the cake carefully to a serving platter, and decorate it with the candied orange peel.
Refrigerate until ready to serve.

ORANGE MOUSSE CAKE WITH ORANGE LIQUEUR

This cake is an impressive-looking dessert, a taste of days gone by.
Should be prepared at least one day before serving.

Ingredients: Cake base: ● Chocolate pastry, 9" in diameter and 1/2 inch thick
● 5 tablespoons brandy ● 5 tablespoons orange liqueur
Chocolate cream: ● 101/2 ounces semi-sweet chocolate, broken into pieces
● 11/2 containers whipping cream ● 3 tablespoons brandy
Orange mousse: ● 1/2 ounce unflavored gelatin ● 1/4 cup boiling water
● 4 egg yolks ● 1/2 cup sugar ● 1/2 cup freshly squeezed orange juice
● 3 tablespoons frozen orange juice concentrate ● 3 tablespoons orange liqueur
● 11/2 containers whipping cream
Decoration: ● orange segments, white membrane removed

9" spring-form baking pan, greased

Preparation:

1. Chocolate cream preparation: Put the chocolate and the cream in a small saucepan and bring to a boil. Remove from the flame, add the brandy and stir until the chocolate melts. Refrigerate for 8 hours.

2. Cake base preparation: Place the chocolate pastry in the baking pan and drizzle the brandy and the ligueur over it. Beat the refrigerated chocolate-cream mixture until firm. Spread over the pastry and refrigerate.

3. Orange mousse preparation: Melt the gelatin in the boiling water. Beat the egg yolks and sugar for 6 minutes until fluffy and shiny pale yellow. Strain the dissolved gelatin into the yolks and mix well.

4. Add the orange juice, orange concentrate and liqueur and mix.

5. Whip the cream until firm and fold gently into the orange mixture. Spoon the whipped cream/orange mixture over the chocolate cream in the pan and refrigerate overnight.

6. Decorate with orange segments before serving

Ice-cream Cake with Meringue Cookies and Nuts

Ingredients: ● 10½ ounces meringue cookies ● 7 ounces chopped, toasted hazelnuts ● 3½ ounces chopped, sugared pecans ● 14½ ounces sweetened, condensed milk ● 2 tablespoons instant coffee powder ● 2 containers whipping cream
Decoration: ● 4 tablespoons sweetened cocoa powder

10″ spring-form baking pan, greased

Preparation:

1. Using a rolling pin crush the meringue cookies into fine crumbs. Add all the nuts, condensed milk and coffee powder.

2. Whip the cream until firm and fold into the nut mixture. Spoon into the pan and freeze overnight. Decorate with the sweetened cocoa powder and serve.

✳ Store the cake in the freezer

DATE AND NUT ROLL

This delicacy is not baked, contains no flour and is suitable for both meat or dairy meals.
It is easy to prepare and suitable for the whole year (Rosh Hashana, because of the honey;
Tu B'shvat, because of the dried fruit, etc)

Ingredients: ● 1 cup chopped, toasted hazelnuts ● 1 cup chopped, toasted almonds
● 1 cup chopped, toasted walnuts or pistachios
● ½ cup honey ● 1 cup sugar ● 1 pound pitted dates
● 2 tablespoons oil, for oiling ● shredded coconut or sesame seeds, for coating

30-40 slices

Preparation:

1. Mix the almonds and other nuts in a bowl. Put the honey, sugar and dates in
a saucepan and cook over a medium heat while stirring until the mixture is uniformly mixed.
Add the mixed nuts and mix. Remove from the flame and refrigerate for 1 hour.

2. Oil a work surface. Form two cylinders from the dough, each 1¼ inches in diameter. Roll each
cylinder in the coconut or the sesame seeds. Wrap in baking paper and freeze for 1 hour.

3. Slice the rolls and arrange on a serving platter and serve. You can store the rolls in the freezer.

Coconut-Sour Cream Cookies

Ingredients: ● 4 egg whites ● 1½ cups sugar ● 2-3 tablespoons potato flour ● 7 ounces shredded coconut ● ⅔ cup sour cream ● 1 teaspoon vanilla extract

2 cookie sheets, covered with greased baking paper

20 cookies

Preparation:

1. Preheat oven to low heat (300 degrees F.). Whip the egg whites with sugar to form very stiff peaks. Fold the potato flour and the coconut gently into the whipped whites.

2. Mix the cream with the vanilla extract, add to the coconut mixture and mix gently.

3. Take a heaping tablespoon of the coconut mixture and place on the greased baking paper-lined pan, and form a mound about 2 inches high with it. Do the same with the remaining batter, leaving 2 inches between each mound.

4. Bake the mounds for one hour until they begin to take on a golden color. Cool, and remove carefully with a spatula.

ALMOND-PINE NUT COOKIES

Ingredients: ● 2 egg whites ● 9 ounces ground, blanched almonds ● 9 ounces powdered sugar
Coating: ● Powdered sugar ● 2 beaten egg whites ● 7 ounces pine nuts

2 cookie sheets, covered with greased baking paper

25 cookies

Preparation:

1. Preheat the oven to high heat (390 degrees F.). Beat the eggs lightly in a bowl. Add the almonds and the powdered sugar and stir until the mixture is uniform and not sticky. If the mixture is too sticky add more ground almonds. If the mixture is too dry add a little more egg white.

2. Dust your hands with powdered sugar, so that the batter will not stick to your hands. Make balls from the nut mixture, coat with the beaten egg whites and then roll in the pine nuts. Place on the baking pan.

3. Bake for 10-15 minutes until the pine nuts begin to take on a golden color. Cool and store in a closed jar.

No BAKE ORANGE BALLS

This recipe is suitable for meat or dairy meals and is highly recommended for Seder night.

Ingredients: ● 3 thick-skinned oranges ● 1 pound sugar ● ½ cup water
● ¼ cup lemon juice ● shredded coconut for decoration (not essential)

About 20 balls

Preparation:

1. Put the oranges in a saucepan, cover with water, bring to a boil and remove from the heat. Allow to sit in the cooking water for fifteen minutes and drain. Replace in the saucepan, cover with water again, bring to a boil and remove from the flame. Let sit for 10 minutes in the cooking water and drain.

2. Cut the oranges into quarters, remove seeds, and grind in a meat grinder.

3. Cook the water (½ cup) and sugar together over a low flame until a thick syrup forms (about 15 minutes).

4. Add the ground oranges and the lemon juice to the syrup and cook, stirring from time to time, until the syrup is absorbed into the oranges and the mixture is very thick (about 50 minutes). Cool well in the refrigerator for a few hours or overnight.

5. Make small balls from the mixture and roll the balls in coconut. Place in fluted paper cups to serve.

CHOCOLATE-COCONUT BALLS WITH ALMOND COATING

These chocolate-coconut balls, coated with toasted almond flakes melt in the mouth, so it is worthwhile to make a double recipe. Prepare this wonderful, no bake delicacy the day before serving

---

Ingredients: ● 9 ounces semi-sweet chocolate, broken into pieces ● 9 ounces butter
● 3 tablespoons sweetened cocoa powder ● 1 tablespoon instant coffee powder
● 2 tablespoons chocolate liqueur or brandy ● 3 eggs
● 5¼ ounces powdered sugar ● 5¼ ounces shredded coconut
Coating: ● 7 ounces flaked, toasted almonds

40 balls

Preparation:

The day before serving

1. Put the chocolate, butter, cocoa, coffee powder and liqueur into a medium saucepan and cook over a low heat until the chocolate melts and the mixture has a uniform consistency. Remove from the flame and cool.

2. Beat the eggs and the powdered sugar until fluffy and pale yellow. Add the chocolate mixture and beat for 1 minute. Add the coconut, mix and refrigerate for 24 hours.

The day of serving

3. Make balls from the mixture, roll in the almond flakes and arrange in fluted paper cups.

CHOCOLATE-BRANDY-NUT TRUFFLES

Rich chocolate-nut balls, coated with cocoa powder. The word "truffle" is derived from the mushroom truffle; the shape of the chocolate ball is like the shape of the truffle.

Ingredients: ● 10½ ounces semi-sweet chocolate chips ● ½ cup whipping cream
● 2 tablespoons brandy ● 3½ ounces softened butter ● 2 egg yolks ● 2 ounces chopped walnuts
● 1 teaspoon Instant coffee powder, for coating ● 30 walnut halves (optional)

30 truffles

Preparation:

1. Put the chocolate, cream and brandy in the top of a small double boiler and heat while stirring with a wooden spoon until the chocolate melts.

2. Remove from the flame and stir in the butter until absorbed into the chocolate.

3. Add the egg yolks, nuts and coffee powder and stir well. Freeze for an hour or more until the mixture has a dough-like consistency.

4. Make 30 balls from the dough and then roll in the cocoa powder. Place in fluted paper cups. You may decorate each ball with a walnut half. Refrigerate until serving.

INDEX

alvah

icolada cake (with white chocolate and halvah mousse) 66

e-cream

e-cream cake with meringue ookies and nuts 78

ams

oppy seed-chocolate cake with cherry (or blueberry) jam and whipped cream 36

iwi

hocolate explosion 46
avlova with whipped cream and fruit 48

emon

Valnut cake with lemon mousse filling 28

ychee

Coconut-lychee cake with whipped cream 34

Mousses

Chocolate walnut cake with chocolate-coffee mousse 64
Coconut-walnut meringue with chocolate mousse 52
Hazelnut cake with white chocolate mousse 62
Orange mousse cake with orange liqueur 76
Praline-nut cake with chocolate mousse 60
Tricolada cake (with white chocolate and halvah mousse) 66
Walnut cake with lemon mousse filling 28

Walnut meringue with chocolate mousse and chocolate balls 58

Nuts

Almond-walnut cake with toffee cream and whipped cream 30
Chocolate-brandy-nut truffles 90
Chocolate-hazelnut-strawberry cake 42
Chocolate walnut cake with chocolate-coffee mousse 64
Coconut-chocolate-raisin-nut torte 14
Coconut-walnut meringue with chocolate mousse 52
Date and nut roll 80
Hazelnut cake with hazelnut cream and white chocolate whipped cream 32
Hazelnut cake with white chocolate mousse 62
Hazelnut meringue with chocolate-caramel creme 54
Ice-cream cake with meringue cookies and nuts 78
Meringue with hazelnut trifle and brandy mocca creme 56
Pastry with coconut-walnut merinque 20
Praline-nut cake with chocolate mousse 60
Walnut cake with cinnamon syrup and creme fraiche 72
Walnut cake with lemon mousse filling 28
Walnut meringue with chocolate mousse and chocolate balls 58
Walnut-whipped cream cake with shaved chocolate 22

Orange

Almond cake with orange syrup 10
Festive chocolate-orange cake 74
No bake orange balls 86

Orange mousse cake with orange liqueur 76
Pavlova with whipped cream and fruit 48

Pine nut

Almond-pine nut cookies 84

Poooy seed

Poppy seed-chocolate cake with cherry jam and whipped cream 36
Rich poppy seed cake with whipped cream and white chocolate 38

Praline

Praline-nut 60

Raisins

Coconut- chocolate-raisin- nut torte 14

Sauces

Vanilla sauce 24

Strawberries

Chocolate-hazelnut-strawberry cake 42
Meringue cake with whipped cream and strawberries 50
Pavlova with whipped cream and fruit 48

Syrups

Amaretto (almond liquer) syrup 18
Brandy syrup 16
Cinnamon syrup 72
Orange syrup 10
Rich sugar syrup 38
Sugar syrup 34

Vanilla

Italian almond cake with vanilla sauce 24
Almond cake with vanilla sauce 26
Vanilla sauce 24

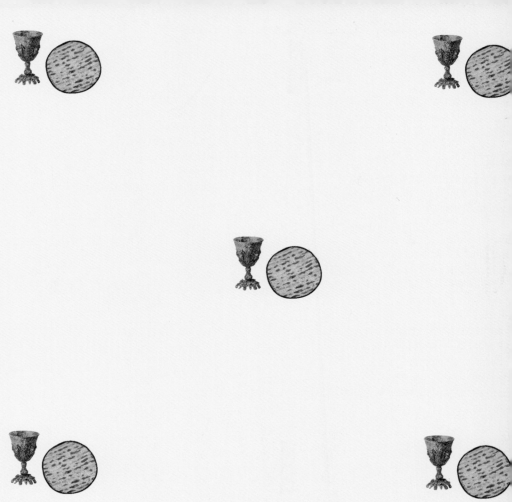